DIRECTION OF THE WEATHER VANE

Poems and Songs

by

Doug Bass

ISBN: 0-9717195-0-0

FOR

CORY, CASEY and MICHELLE

"You don't need a weatherman
to know which way the wind blows"

BOB DYLAN

CONTENTS

KODIAK POEMS

NO PROMISES

Let's dance dear one
Down by the sea
'Neath warm blue moon
Wine flowing free

Walk hidden shore
Not knowing end
Let's chance some more
Around the bend

Each turn we take
Each spin of dance
True love? Forsake?
It's in the chance

But let's hold our promises
Back tonight
They're easy coming
When all is right

LET US NEVER FORGET

Something there that no one knows.
Something there that cannot be explained.
Something deeper than deep sleep.
Something deeper than deep subconscious.
Something within the sea.
Something within the electron.
Something within total devotion
flying beautifully on the wind of fate.
Something deeper than deep.

—a spider spinning its web—
—a giant redwood tree—
—a hard brown seed—
—a planet orbiting—
—a dying face smiling—
—total devotion flying—

Something there that cannot be explained.
Something deeper than deep.

THOUGHTS IN A BAR

There you are
Down there at the other end of the bar
You're not a hooker
You look too concerned staring into the wine
Something heavy is on your mind

I wish I could reach you
I wish I could talk to you
But there's too much that separates us
                that puts you away too far:
Fourteen ashtrays and thirty feet of bar

That's too thick a wall for me to break through
We could hurdle that wall with our eyes
But you won't look—and look
        is as far as I'll go:
I never was a player at the mashing game

So we'll stay on our separate ends
In our separate worlds
                worlds apart too far
And though it seems you are light years away
It's only fourteen ashtrays and thirty feet of bar

Confining us to solitude

THE RECITAL

On the walls, old prints of beautiful nude women.
The lines of these women never grew old.
On the floor, sawdust and peanut shells.
In the air, smoke and holiday voices.

It was a circular bar there,
Where we were all singing old standards, old songs,
While an organ player in the middle
Worked hard at his job to mesmerize us
        into singing and buying and singing and buying
All night long.

Most of the flock were following the shepherd.
Request came constantly.
Some guy asked for a Christmas song
        and the organist played "O Holy Night".
After it was over the guy said,
        "Where the hell's that Christmas song?!"
And he meant it.
He kept talking to himself all night.
I guess he was talking to somebody
        he thought was there.

It started snowing and a girl from Georgia
        (who had just arrived in Kodiak not long ago)
said, "Oh! Is that snow?!"
An answer came quick,
        "No, it's grits."

The organist kept working
        and trying to please and appease
                and ingratiate all in the circle.
Though the words of the seasonal songs
        celebrated good will and cheer,
There was a subtle nuance one could hear
                in some of the voices:
        the sound of five thousand heartaches breaking.

continued . . .

Now the organist is questioning me,
    trying to humor me
    so to pry open my wallet with the teeth he smiles with.

I leave the circle
    and walk out into the frozen night.
Another world.
The organist is cut out.
Loneliness wears no frills now.
My footsteps squeak in the snow as I walk to my car,
        creating an abstract kind of music:
    Rhythm and Boots,
        the sound of five thousand snowflakes breaking.

The moon takes my attention
    and holds it more strongly
        than the organist did.

Back to the sounds of silence again,
Wondering in my own private world
Why and how and why
And now it feels like
    five thousand questions waking.

Vietnam is still raging, still afire.
Alaska has just recently had an earthquake.
The organist is still playing,
Empty hearts are being filled with perishable sweets.
A mesmerized coyote is howling at the moon,
And a politician is telling everyone
    what it's all about.

OF SEA AND MAN

The sea takes on many moods
And hides buried many secrets
        beneath many faces.
It puts me in mind of human mind.
The glass today
        is swells tomorrow
                are changing colors
                        by the hour
                                by sun's viewpoint.

The sea follows the moon,
        lives with the pull,
                runs from the wind,
                        lives with the push, and
Maintains the personality
        that runs the spectrum of man's mind:
Lives in spite of us.

The sea can rock and breathe you to sleep
        with a whisper song
Or reflect the anger of sky and wind,
And your blood will run wild
To match the moment.

The sea lives by the moon.
We live by the sea.
Does the sea put me in mind
                of human mind?

No, after reconsidering,
Human mind reminds me of the sea:
You know, heredity.

COMBINATIONS

White, misty ghosts being windswept
        across a raging bay,
Appearing and disappearing.

Snappy, rushing waves pounding black rocks
        and the mountain wind
                impetuous and ruthless.

A whirling, dancing snow funnel
        rises, crosses the road,
And destroys itself against a warehouse.

"Storms in Africa" comes on the radio
And I watch a sea gull hang in the air
        facing wind and sunset
                behind dark mountains.

Clouds catch fire hanging over the sun,
The wind and sea rage on,
"Storms in Africa" is still playing,
My mind hangs in the air,
My heart rages,
And I nearly cry.

• • • • • • • • • •

Epilogue

The song goes off,
        gull flies away,
                sun drops and clouds cool to darkness,
                        someone walks in,
                                and the phone rings.

THE DAY I TEMPORARILY LOST MY LIFE IN ALASKA AND LOVED EVERY MINUTE OF IT

The sad, wise
        black eyes
Of a little Indian girl in Alaska
        tore my heart right out
Faster than anything else
        ever has in my life.

I can still see her
With the yellow Buttercup
        in her hair,
And I am hers,
Balanced beautifully
        somewhere between
                her melancholy eyes
And tooth missing smile.

If I could hug her,
My life would not be mine,
But Life
        would open another bloom.

WANDERLUST

Morning was cool and clear
  and blue-gray clouds strung
    'cross the sky
  with red edges facing the Eastern horizon.

Ice lilies cuddled together near
    the shore and 'round the pier,
  except for a few the current caught and
    set free to float away,
      journey the bay.
Gulls flew around in slow circles
    on light wings and
  hung in the air for easy moments
Playing the wind for their next turn.

(My heart was light
and wanted to fly away
over the white mountains,
or float around the channel
    out to sea)

We threw off the hawser lines
And the tug boats signaled to the ship
And the ship blasted its
    air shattering response.

Then the ship drifted away
Around the channel,
Out of sight,
Out to sea.

I went about my regular job
Doing it mechanically,
For I was somewhere else.

GOD'S WORKSHOP

The waves charge in,
        angry, slamming, determined
And crash against bold, gray, jagged rocks
Rocks that crumble to sand
        after eternities of ruthless sea attacks.

But that is life stirring,
Life crying and jerking impulsively in its birth.
The sea is God's workshop,
And the slamming and banging and roaring
Is the sound of something being made.

Look to the sea
And its secrets are so deep
        you will shiver with wonder,
And its will is so strong
        you will know it's alive.

Every time the sea meets the rocks
It is destroyed into upshots
                of salty mists,
Mists that jump on the iron faces of the rocks
                and do what they can.
But give the sea a million years to work
And the rocks will be sand,
With waves rolling over
Easily.

Do you feel a kinship to the sea?
Do you gaze at and through the waves,
        on and on 'til you see your mind?

Do you sometimes look backwards,
                beyond memory,
Back to the mists of your mind,
The salty mists that had a will so strong
        they wouldn't be defeated
By bold, gray, jagged rocks?

SNOWSTORM

It started meekly before the day'd turned light
As I was driving home after a date that night.
I thought little of it, but noticed it was sticking
On the frozen ground
And the wind was picking
Up the dry snow and swirling it around.

I crawled into bed knowing it was snowing,
I slept warm and sound—the wind kept blowing.
While jeweled sculptures danced down through the air,
I turned and I tossed
In dreams, unaware.
I was home in sleep—in sleep I was lost.

It was not 'til I woke that it really got bad,
But I made it to work and of that I was glad.
All day long winter slammed with much might—
The wind sang a song
But the song had a bite
You could feel in your bones.

Darkness fell and I had to go eat,
But I didn't realize I would have to compete
With the raging storm with a will of its own.
My car was ice packed
And the wind was still blowin'—
I pulled hard on the door and the ice cracked.

Before I could sit down I was blown off my feet
And a snow funnel dancing colored white my car seat.
They say Hell is fire—this storm was ice,
But this storm I tell you
Was not Heaven's device.
The Master of the World was the raging white blue.

It ended meekly before the day'd turned light
As I was thawing out after working that night.
I saw frosty patterns as I stared through the window,
Saw a ghost moon
And etchings of wind blow,
And knew I'd been humbled by Hell's Ice Platoon.

LOVE AND OTHER FIRES

DIRECTION OF THE WEATHER VANE

A rare July cool front
moved in
And lay gently across the land.
The clouds, slow, friendly,
came down dripping,
releasing easy mist,
Touching the tree tops,
washing the wooded hills.

It sparked an old memory into
breathing again
And I was back in the Island days.

It all came back,
The frantic and hurried
embrace of new love,
The immediacy of the need
consuming,
A wind blown prairie fire
saying,
"If we don't love right now,
The species may die out!"

But for the cooling rains and mists,
We may very well have burned the Island
Off the face of the sea.

KISSES

At first, landing so soft
Barely perceptible
        like hot little snowflakes
(if you can imagine such a thing)

Then somehow someway
                somewhere in those kisses

        lightning became involved

And those hot little snowflakes
        became an avalanche
Taking me, sweeping me away

TUNNEL OF LOVE

The darkness doesn't scare me
The entrance, Heaven's Gate
Inside it's back to Eden
Like Eden, I can't stay

But when the journey's over
I wonder—(It's no guess)
Is life worth reaffirming?
The answer: Yes! Yes! Yes!

FALLING

First off, she carded me
That didn't hurt things any
Maybe she was just being nice or maybe
        she just knew what was good for business:
It was good for mine

And then her eyes
Dark and bright at the same instant
What is so alluring about a black flame?
        a hot velvet midnight? Her eyes were such

And then her lovely, lively ass
It binds me in a spell
I stare like a stalking cat
She must notice
        but I don't care
It's not just me
I look around the room
        and see others staring too:
What a glorious ass!

She wears a little too much perfume around
        her neck and ear area
But it's not choking and not too bad
And it's strangely appealing that
        she just doesn't know better yet
It makes me curious to smell around
        and see if she goes heavy with it
                everywhere

Her mouth I would like to fill
        with my tongue or else . . .
It is a pretty mouth, a sexy mouth
One with a purpose:
        to give or take

Yet, while her mouth has a primitive
        and profound affect upon me,

continued . . .

A quick, surprising balance comes
    when sunlit laughter dances out
        slinging flowers around the room

And then she looks at me
And the black flame consumes

She moves quick
She talks quick
She looks quick and laughs quick
And her very walk is a dance

And I sit heavily,
    slowly wanting her.

DARK NIGHT

When the night comes
        everything changes
And you do—too.

Daily concerns sink out of sight
And up comes, up comes those
        undeniable first little crocuses of desire
Growing along the banks of River Eden.

And once removed from the fierce, brutal
Bustin' busy light of hit and hustle day,
There's no getting away from
                The need for connection
                        The human touch,
Needing love like needing to breathe.

Every night is the same: Do you find it
                (and live)
Or do you sit, still and grim,
        a naked tortured soul,
Wanting to—But instead

Sit and stare at a mindless bar TV
Sledgehammering your brain into the
        murky Whiskey River,

Trying so desperately
                        to douse the fire
                that wants to light up the night.

I've no regrets you fled away
From what we had or were
You flew away
You flew away
But I've no regrets
Oh sure
I missed you then
Think of you now
But I've no regrets
Oh no!

I've no regrets you turned away
And let the story close,
You threw away
You threw away
I accept the end you chose
And yes
It hurt back then
Remember when?
But I've no regrets
Oh no!

Back then the clock moved slow and fuzzed
Through urgent hungry tears,
Twas just a passing breeze
You know?
You know,
It seemed like years.
Twas so nice I found you then,
So natural to lose you too
And I've no regrets today you know,
No regrets—do you?

• • • • • • • • • •

I was in the Spring of my years,
A wild and raging river out of its banks.

continued . . .

It was not love, no,
It was only the Earth turning.

I didn't want to wed you,
I only wanted to flood you—wash through
You again and again
Breathing a rhythmic YES! To LIFE
    Til your heart was afloat in my seed.

That's all it was,
And there's no regrets, there's no regrets
No, there's no regrets—Oh no!

ONCE

Once I knew you, girl
Once we talked with true tongues
Once we let our guards down
Once I loved you, girl
And you swore you loved me, too

We knew each other's eyes
We knew each other's dreams
We knew the scent of each other's heat
Once I loved you, girl

Once used to be now
Now, once is used to be

Once I knew you, girl
Once I loved you, girl

Once   Once   Once

STILL

Even though
You are far away
Out of sight, out of reach

Even so
Every day
I still see you
You still touch me

AN OLD, OLD STORY

Fog and moonlight and late air
Played on the world one night
As night bugs sung an infinite song
To accompany the sight

A girl was with me and I smelled her perfume
By the evergreen I kissed her
I felt warmth and love that fit just right
In an old, old story
In the ghost kissed night

We stood there awhile
I know not how long
There in the moonlight and fog
And the night bugs sung an infinite song

SUNSET DOOR

Day is boxed in action
Though with light, All can see
Night is opened up mystery
And all things gone
            to infinity

That is why I say
That night is bigger than day
Day holds life, 'tis so
But night holds life
            bigger than life we know

ANOTHER QUESTION ON A WINTER DAY

A tree stood tall
        its bare limbs made patterns
        against white and blue sky interwoven
                a blanket knit by mist angels.

Tree, why do your patterns design
        the picture of reach?
Why are you reaching for that
        white and blue blanket
                spread from all horizons to
All horizons?

ANOTHER QUESTION ON A COLD SPRING DAY

Broken bows,
            yellow sad hair
River dried up,
            honey bees not there
Something is amiss

Fireflies, clean skies
            where did you go?
The mall on the meadow
            the yellow back hoe
Belching progress's kiss

Broken promises,
            a rutted red stare
Rush any direction,
            bottom line waits you there
Where are we going?

This is not to bemoan all the
            new things I've seen, but
There once was a time for the
            dandelion and daydream
What seeds are we sowing?

PROJECTION

Brown star of leaf falling
Now slave of gravity and fickle wind
But once slave to hold of tree
Do you know where you're going?

When you hit the ground
        after your impetuous teeter-totter path down
Do you know where you'll be?
Will you forget the tree
        when snow buries you with cool crystals?

And as I sit watching smoke rise
        from burning coal that holds my eyes
I wonder:
Brown star of leaf falling
Do you know where you're going?

The coal laughs a crackle
                and drops red stars glowing
And I sit and wonder:
Where am I going?

DRIP DROPS

Singularly, it means not much
Hardly worth a glance of note
A time or two, here and there
The consequence—remote

But a touch of love, or absence of
Will build, weigh and define
Like a drip that falls upon a rock
Carving out its own design

The tick of a clock, an hour, a day
They pass hardly noticed at all
But accumulatively, they sum up a life
Til the clock's final tick on the wall

As the poet said, 'twas the road not taken
Made all the difference, eventually
As each day adds a drop, what was done
what was not
How a life is defined, singularly.

TUNED IN

All through the day
I'd hear voices, voices
Telling me how to find the way

All through the night
I'd hear voices, voices
Telling me how to find the light

This morn I awoke
        to hear the wind blow,
                wind blow
Away the confusion
        the voices
                the yoke

What I heard wasn't wrong
It was music, music
From within
        my own voice
                the spirit
                        a song

NEVER FAR FROM HOME

The Isle of the Bear,
        the crashing waves,
The roaring and rumbling sea . . .
Alaskan water rolling over the sand
Was vaguely familiar to me . . .
Where had I heard this before?
        I know!

    An uneasy sleep
    A hot July night,
    All was so eerily still . . .
    Then the crashing and roaring
            and rumbling thunder
    Rolled over those Hacker Creek hills.

I sat at night on Daytona Beach
Listening, and breathing the sea.
The vast expanse
        and the secret depths
Sang hits of eternity . . .
I felt I had sat there before.
        I know!

    I sat as a boy
            on Dad's garage roof
    Peering through summer night skies.
    The pin points of light
            sparked a wonder within
    And eternity poured into my eyes.

A Wyoming wind blew in a new love,
(But how can this old road be new?)
My legs felt sixteen,
        all the colors were freshened,
And I believed what I felt was true . . .
Where had I felt this before?
        I know!

continued . . .

The smell of bubble gum
    and too much perfume,
Innocence taking a dare.
High School hearts
    pounding life's drums
At the old drive-in theater World's Fair.

Change the scenery, change the names,
The labels all just fall away.
There is something that binds
    the past to the present,
That anchors the night to the day . . .
I always feel I've been here before.
    You know?

No matter the slant
    of my inclinations
Or distance
    or directions I roam,
Inevitably, I come face to face
    with my Indiana home.

THE OLD MAIN STREET DRIVE-IN THEATER: AN IMPRESSION

Moonlit skin,
Bubble gum breath,
Perfumed hair,
Eyes of wonder and fire.

I had never heard
        anything as musical
                as your soft laugh,
I had never seen
        anything as beautiful
                as your bare breasts.

There was nothing else
                I could do
But ask you to go steady.

WYOMING WIND

A Wyoming wind sweeps the sky clean.
A crystal, silver cloud brushes by sun
    and a spectrum of color makes rainbow border.

Casper mountain, natural monument of beauty,
    holding shade, water, and life.
Its form creates feelings
    from morning to eve
        with shadow and light.

And the mountain, building toward the heavens,
    waits for the first kiss of October snow.
Down below,
The gold autumn leaves
    flicker light
        and gauge the breeze.

I feel the strange combination
    of clean energy and fulfillment
        with pure, deep loneliness;
Living with a natural need.

As the October sun crosses a clear, deep sky
And the shadows move mountains
        through form and color,
I say: Blow, Wyoming wind, blow!
Blow with clean energy,
Blow to fulfillment,
Blow with a natural need.

HOMECOMING

Home from my labor
Uneasy, unsung
Feel I must do something
Something's left undone

Like worms in my stomach
Like ants in my brain
Like the anxious silence
'fore lightning and rain

Can't find peace
In the moment at hand
In the silence of silence
In the sound of a band

But the sweet wine of love
Fills up my head
As I lie near the sun
Next to you in our bed

Then the calm comes
You're warm 'gainst my back
My heart fills with heat
Pushing out the deep black

The baby kicks softly
Like lightning afar
The promise of rain
And sunshine tomorrow

I smile to myself
At the storm yet to come
High on the challenge
Of what's left undone

REQUEST FOR A MASSAGE

Massage my feet
Massage my brain
Massage my balls
Massage my fame

Massage me up
Massage me down
Massage me flat
Massage me round

Massage my hair
Massage my bones
Massage my blood
Massage my clones

Massage my ego
Massage my id
Massage my old
Massage my kid

THE RACE

Rows and chains of clouds hurry past the moon
So bright and clean,
Not even stopping a moment to notice,
Or taste a lovely beam.
The clouds race on, clawing, tearing and grasping
All the way through the night,
Toward the darkness and horizon
Away from the moon's true light.

THE COMMON TRAP

Hard physical work
        only leads one to
More hard physical work

And gains one a reputation
        of being a good
Hard physical worker

As one sweats through
        the downward muscle spiral
                to the grave.

OUTSIDE INSIDE

Crying, barking, and whining of dogs
Drew my ears from dialogue
My eyes were fixed upon.
Then silence fell and I returned
To book again, I was concerned
How plot would carry on.

The barking filled my ears once more,
And I faced the night and chore
Of leaving warmth and story line
To check the cause of cry and whine.

The moon lit all, all I could see
To find what might the trouble be.
And from chance there might be danger
I look around for prowling stranger.

What trouble? What the dogs had borne,
What caused their crying so forlorn?
One dog had been adventuresome,
His journey led to little fun.
Outside of the fence was he
And on the inside, lonely she.

AND GOD GAVE US DREAMS

A dream is one thing
One can entertain
And raise hell with
And shed all morals
One pretends to have
When releasing selective behavior
Before others' eyes.
It is the one thing
One can do all this with
And not worry
About getting raided by the cops
Or rejected
Or ostracized
Or shunned
Or maimed
Or gossiped about.
Let us thank God
For giving us
The capacity to dream
So we can entertain
Our grossest sins
In hiding
From mans'
Relentless
Merciless
Unforgiving
Accusing
Sadistic eyes.

I AM AN ARTIST

You know
Me and Michelangelo
We go back a long way
            You know?

He may be a bolt
            of lightning
And I just a static glitch

But we're made of
            the same Stuff
      You know?

Me and Michelangelo

THE MAGIC IN THE MIRACLE

Had it only happened just one time
Existence—a one act play
The Dawn and the story unfolding til Dusk
And say then it was called a Day

That in itself would be so much more
Than a mind could comprehend:
That the curtain rose on a miracle
Then the curtain fell at the end

Had the Earth in its orbit made but one trip around
Rolling Life through its turns til Fall
Who would not be astounded
By the depth and the breadth of it all?

And yet Autumn, sweet harvest—a firestorm of color
Informs a much deeper need
Incinerating a season
While delivering up the seed

That we're here at all is a miracle
(Rejoice! Laugh! Dance! and Sing!)
But to lie down to sleep and to rise again
We're talking a different thing

The landscape of Autumn—a powerful beauty!
But the little brown seed is the thing:
Locked safe in the dark, it harbors the spark
To ignite the creation of Spring!

RESOLVE

I didn't want to fool with it this year.
Just too much trouble.
Night dogs trampling through
        freshly planted soil.
Too little rain, too much rain.
Bugs, apparently starved
        until they discovered my garden.
And the onslaught of weeds.
And again and again the weeds.

Yes, I was just going to forget about it,
    give the soil rest, myself rest.
After all, I could buy nice fruits and vegetables
    at a roadside stand for little money
        and no bother.

Then those first two or three days hit when
Everything alive knows there is
Something going on.
Something inside me gently snapped
And the mental armies I thought I had on red alert
        to resist breaking ground
Had all quickly and silently deserted.
There would be no war.
There was nothing I could do.

I walked, resolved, to check the tiller in the shed.

HARD SPRING FALL

One late but humorless frost
passing through the county late
One night,
lay waste thirty days tending with
One Judas kiss.

The following morning,
all bright and boastful,
Salts the wound with the laughter
of birds and the mocking smile
Of healthy dandelions.

The plants are still there
in their places,
But nothing is happening
anymore.
The weeds are still
growing,
Hummingbirds
and butterflies
busy about,
But nothing is happening
anymore.
The moon is still in
its sky,
The sun warms the Earth
by day,
But the fence that circles
the garden
Is a necklace around
a corpse,
For nothing is happening
anymore.

• • • • • • • • • •

Bittersweet lullaby,
A not-wanting-to, bad
good-bye.
Needed sleep
will not come,
Fear what morn
will find undone.
Purpose served,
the seed is spent,
Wonder where
the summer went?
The sky above,
the soil below,

continued . . .

'Tis still the same
but love does slow.
In its cage,
the garden's still.
I watch it from
my window sill.
The years I worked it,
the irony!
Now I feel it
work in me.

AUTUMN STORM

The hold weakens,
then is through,
And gravity pulls the leaves home.
I pull them together with rake
'til all is nice and neat.
"I'll work them into the garden", I think.
But while I'm thinking
and not looking
A storm the TV gave no warning of
breaks fast and furious
and lay flat and wide
and scattered what
was nice and neat.

The kids . . .
performing their autumn ritual.
I'm tempted to scold,
but for what?
I'd do as much good scolding the milkweed
for letting loose its silky snow,
releasing tomorrow on the wind.

Kids . . .
It looks like
they're just having fun,
But is there something deep within
the nature of their play
that knows leaves, after all,
are supposed to be scattered?

A WALK IN THE GARDEN

You say you wonder
        at the naivete of my belief?

Come with me.

Here is my garden—Now
        take off your shoes.

Walk over this way—Feel
        the Earth embrace your feet.
Feel the Life, the Potential,
        the Kinetic Energy—Feel
        your eyes dilate with wonder.

Now walk over this way.
Pick this warm, red globe
        and feel it in your hand—The
Red from the Earth and the Warmth from
        ninety three million miles away.

Now take this miraculous accident of
        Sodium and Chloride hooking up
And sprinkle it there
        where you licked a wet spot.
And now, and now—taste!

(Oh mercy, sweet Lord, oh mercy!
How better to explain?)

I see you enjoy the fruit
        but are not convinced
                and are still amused
                        at my lack of depth.

I admit, I am sure
        I will never be smart enough
To be an atheist.

Pass the salt, please.

POTATO PLANTIN'

Now I've peeled a heap of taters
Ate heaps my whole life through
But I'd not much knowin'
    on when to plant
An' what you're s'posed to do.

So I inquired of a farmer friend
Hopin' to learn the fact
He said, "I'll help you out!"
    and handed me
This years almanac.

I read a bit, but then I quit
I just couldn't quite believe
A book filled with astrology
And future teller's weave

But then I dug up a legend
    from the Rio Grande
That was stored on the edge of my brain
I heard it sometime, somewhere
    in my past
While headin' north on a train.

"Get a bottle of Mescal!", so legend goes
"Get the biggest one you can find.
Get a sack of lemons and a shaker of salt
And drink til you're nearly blind.

"When the bottle's near dry
    look the worm in the eye
And show him the edge of a tooth
Say, 'Tell me no lies to the questions I ask—
I'll eat you for less than the truth!'.

"Then ask away for the whole of the day
He'll tell you your fill of the head

continued . . .

Though you'll learn what you seek
it'll take you a week
To heal your Mescal head."

Well folks, that's how it started and how I come to find out all about potato plantin'. Yes, I decided to give legend a try. So I set aside two week-end days (and nights) just for myself. I was takin' no calls, answering no doors, beeps, rings, buzzers, or bells of anykind. I took a large bottle of Mescal (with the worm) and salt and lemons to the back room and locked myself in. There was nothin' left for me to do then but drink.

And that I did
'Til I was damn near out my head
That's when I asked the worm
And this is what he said:

Plant 'em when it's hot
Plant 'em when it's dry
From the first of the month of May
To the first day of July

Plant 'em under dirt
Plant 'em under straw
Under needles of pine
Under dust from the saw

Plant 'em on your birthday
While singin' a tune
While wearin' your hat
That was made from a coon

Plant 'em when the frogs start
To sing up the night
Or on the first day after
The first skeeter bite

Plant 'em when the blues
Got you wearin' a frown
An' you feel like you're the one
Who's underground

continued . . .

Plant 'em after whiskey
Makes your nerves feel like jello
After bee stings make your face look like
A bag of marshmellows

Plant 'em when you're out of bread
And a guitar string breaks
An' the bills come due an' the tax man too
An' your brain surgeon shakes.

Plant 'em when dandelions
Offer their wine
Plant 'em when the bluegill strikes
And straightens your line

Plant 'em when the maple leaves
Start layin' some shade
And the eyesore out your back door
Is startin' to fade

Plant 'em when your mother-in-law
Decides to move in
Plant 'em when your wife
Kicks her back out again

Plant 'em when mornin's brewin'
And the coffee is too
Plant 'em when the night's a fallin'
And beer is the brew

Now you probably wonder
What this has to do with plantin'
All this unrelated rhyme
And riddleotic chantin'

'Tis I, the worm, whose voice you hear
And what I tell is true
Still, I am bottled and you're bagged
The voice just might be you

But if you really want to know
I'll gladly tell you

continued . . .

In easy, simple, plain spoke words
You won't misconstrue

Plant 'em under high noon
        under high moon of midnight
What I'm sayin' friend is plant them when
You damn well like.

APOLOGY

When I was a small child
I remember waking on winter mornings
And seeing a fresh blanket of deep, white snow
inviting me outside.
Perfect beauty, untouched.
Virgin soft cover of cool white.
I couldn't stand it.
I had to run outside and put my footprints
everywhere
And make a mess of the whole picture,
sorta hoping I'd sink up to my neck.
I wanted inside that kind of beauty.
I think that's why I bit your breast last night.

HIGH THUNDER AND YELLOW GREEN SKY

It was a high thunder and yellow green sky. Trouble.
For sure.
At least, to me, that's how it looked.
But what the hell do I know?

Soon enough, sure enough,
it started raining.
But OH MY GOD! OH MY GOD!—
It was raining $100.00 bills!

Don't know how or why or where from,
But spent the rest of my day
becoming rich.

I've since retired—
only from work.
Now it's run and fun and sun
And song and love, smoke and rum,
And cold cold beer.

But I still keep an ear
And keep an eye
For a high high thunder
and a yellow green sky. Trouble?
Maybe.
Or it just might rain
$100.00 bills again.
One never knows about those things.

THAT NIGHT THAT MORNING

I know a knife has cut your mind
And let out things that know no time
And maybe things that know no crime
Appearing in the blue
And you will too
And be and be and be and be, never knowing
Why or needing to.

• • • • • • • • • •

Dancing half sober at the VFW with
A woman half drunk I barely knew
And her perfumed all up,
Singing, flinging, bitter.
The Pledge of Allegiance ringing on the wall
on
every
turn
Flying by my eyes.

Mr. Veteran of Foreign War was there
Said the GIs fought for liberty
And he was taking his, By God!
And it was nobody's business
'Cause his wife and kids were well fed.
One nation under God.
The beer was good.

• • • • • • • • • •

Woke up amazed
At the old type formal poetry
Flying through my brain so fast
I didn't understand any of it.
All I could do was enjoy it.

TO LOVE A DITCH DIGGER

One summer while digging ditches in Indianapolis,
A pretty young lady walked by where our crew labored
And I said "Hi" to her.
She looked at me in my baggy, faded pants and
Sweat wet shirt and
Me with a hot red face and dusty hair and eyebrows and
Dirt streaks on my neck and arms
And she walked on without saying "Hi".

Another day that summer a little girl
With freckles and a tooth out
Played in her yard while we worked in the street.
I said "Hi" to her and smiled with dust around my lips.
She smiled and brought a paper necklace to give me.
The next day she kissed me on my sweaty face
When she asked me to lean down to her a minute.
The next day our crew pulled out
And she cried real hard.

QUESTIONING SILENCE

The daylight loses itself somewhere behind the hill
And the night silence asks, "Why is all so still?"
After the autumn leaves have fallen,
The silent winter asks, "Where did life go?"
The guns are fired and war is waged,
And the silent, glazed eyes of a dead soldier
Asks, "Why does lead go to hearts?"
Bitter words are spoken and hate is felt,
And the silence that follows
Asks, "Where has love gone?"
Time passes quickly in the shadows of the world
And the silence in old age asks,
"Where has everything gone?"

Silence questions all,
But just when it seems
        the questions
Come near being swallowed
        by that very silence
The questions were born of—Rendered mute
    to ask no more

    Just then

    The sun rises
    Spring breaks
    Peace comes
    A new love is found
    A child is born in answer to the claim
    Of a new grave,

And questioning silence just goes on
    Questioning
        Questioning
            Questioning

PASSING THE FIRE

Those warm and palmed volcano days
Is there no vestige left?
An Eden, rich, but out of reach,
From which we're left bereft?

Nothing is old, nothing is new
It's all been around forever.
They say you can't go back, 'tis true,
But the past will leave you never.

That ancient fire is evermore,
It is a circular thing.
Creation turns through Autumn song
Rounds winter into Spring.

To learn the past, 'tis good indeed!
To know, remember the story.
'Tis right, in fact a duty to
Pay tribute, honor the glory.

But human spirit that rose to meet
Dark forces loosed on the land,
Is not entombed in history books,
Or steps washed from the sand.

Those voyagers of yesterday
Brought us to here and now.
It happened not by accident, they
Had to imagine how.

(Imagine how! Imagine how
The world would be without
Imagination as a tool:
Stagnant, racked in doubt.)

To honor them requires more
Than statues, tributes, tears,

continued . . .

More than learning, remembering, or
A reenactment of those years.

To honor past full and complete
The fire must pass through.
That old fire burns no less today;
You know, you feel, don't you?

To give the past its rightful due,
The torch must ever stay lit,
To forge tomorrow by giving the fire
Of imagination to it.

TIME PIECES

BEFORE AND AFTER

I asked a man once
What was the difference
Between the time before you are born
And the time after you die—He said:

"Well, before you are born,
You aren't
And you never have been.

After you die,
You aren't
But you have been.

And I don't know
If the HAVE BEEN
Between the AREN'Ts
Makes a whole helluva lot of difference
Between the nature of the two aren'ts."

He didn't really answer my question,
But I didn't expect him to.

STRANGELY OUT OF TIME

Gifts come
  sometimes
Strangely out of time

A man of 20 can
  talk as if he's lived
    1000 years
And a man of 80 can
  float toy sail boats
    in the park
And make children feel at home.

But sometimes
  the 1000 year man
    sings of sailing boats
      in the park
        and children laughing.

Sometimes
  gifts come strangely
    out of time.

COLUMBUS DAY

Whoever gets the credit,
Whoever gets the blame,
Whichever way you spin it,
 the truth is still the same.
It would have happened, happened, happened,
 over and over again.

Man reached out to the East,
Man reached out to the West,
Bound to find his destiny,
 born to leave his nest.

When Chris first saw the island,
The roll of waves on the shelf,
"That's you in the mirror!" it was telling him,
 as the world was meeting itself.
And it will happen, happen, happen,
  over and over again.

THE FIRST TIME

We were freshmen, my friend and I
and just had to know
So decided to go
to the whorehouse
Over by the County Seat—
just a stones throw from Law and Order.

We went in. There was not much said
It was dark but for the red glowing at
the end of a cigarette
Held by a man who said only "Hello"
As he listened to the blues
on a radio
Glowing yellow dimly there.
Without a word we knew:
He ran the radio—He ran the show.

Dark, Illegal, Dangerous, Immoral—
My heartbeat could've wrecked a polygraph
As adrenalin raged loose—wild—giddy.

Everything about the place
was old, discolored and dingy
But the Lady who led me away—away she led
Was a siren bursting with beauty!
God, what a smile! (An apple? A serpent? The
Fruit of the Tree of the Knowledge of Good and
Evil? No it was just her Smile, passed on from
Eden, igniting my soul, Life's fountain, my body.)

No use describing what followed then
Just as soon say the tide came in
But common old story though it may be
I remember after many a year—The
Lady who led me away—away she led and

If she was a fallen Angel, I'm
glad she fell my way

continued . . .

And if I were to be kicked from The Garden, I'd
soon it be with her,
Prefer that lusty fiery life to
Staying in
The Garden
with some
thin lipped
virginal, tightassed
Ice Queen.

A NIGHT OUT, TEN YEARS AFTER

Did you think it was over,
'cause they stopped singin' your song?
'cause the name of the band changed
Did you think it was wrong?

Did you really think God
        would destroy 'em for changin',
For comin' and doin'
        their own rearrangin'?

Did you think 'cause they're dancin'
        to new beats of new legends
That God would get angry
        and send Armageddon?

Did you think the world
        would stop livin' when you did?
Did you think after your sale
        there'd be not a new bid?

Did you think it a sin
        to put on a false face,
When the mask that you wore
        was a trip to no place?

Did you really think free kids
        would bow at your feet,
When you turned gray and forty
        riding in the back seat?

Did you think all your friends
        would be here tonight
And applaud at your entrance,
        turn on a spotlight?

Did the beer pick you up
        when the trip put you down
Where you know you're a stranger
        in your own home town?

WHILE I SLEPT

My brain and lips not yet
able to form the words,
Yet the Will to Live was flying high
on a banner singing out to the world
with every heartbeat, Yes! Yes!

I was changing fast.
The world outside was changing direction.
With sacrifice beyond understanding
Hitler and the final solution
were being told, No! No!

One hundred and thirty one days into gestation,
little did I know.
It was only important that my mother
eat and breathe and not shoot up
and not perform some coat hanger handiwork,
Not contact some back alley back room terminator.

I was warm and safe
preparing to land in a world being altered
on a faraway bloody beach.
Paving my way through bullets and fire
and hell and death were young men who were
Where I was—just a few short eighteen, nineteen,
twenty years before.

It was June 6, 1944,
One hundred and thirty one days into gestation.
And while I slept the world

Was deciding whether or not to be Free.

TIME WILL TAKE CARE OF EVERYTHING

YOUNG MAN: Oh, pity me! My heart is broken! My true love has left me for another and I'm so alone and empty. And my money is all gone, too!

OLD MAN: Don't destroy yourself with self-pity and worry, my boy! Time will take care of everything. You will see. When you've seen a lot of time carry men through the forest of living, you'll know what time can do. You'll see.

YOUNG MAN: How can my believing that ease this pain in my soul now? I feel I want to die. Time is so slow.

OLD MAN: But time does pass.

YOUNG MAN: But it crawls; it doesn't fly.

OLD MAN: It crawls with pain; it flies with pleasure—but it always moves and heals. Time will take care of everything. You'll see.

YOUNG MAN: When will I see? I want this thorn plucked from my heart now! When will I see?!

OLD MAN: I cannot say—except, that, you will see. And if the thorn was plucked from your heart now, your heart would be no wiser than before.

YOUNG MAN: Who ever heard of a wise heart?

OLD MAN: The heart is the seat of wisdom. That thorn pricked your heart and woke it.

YOUNG MAN: Wisdom lies in the brain.

OLD MAN: Would you want a family of man with brains and no heart? The heart is where love and tolerance and empathy are learned. And these are the pillars of wisdom.

YOUNG MAN: I have no more love. And you say I'll be wiser?

OLD MAN: You have lost her love, not yours.

YOUNG MAN: I'm empty. I've lost everything.

OLD MAN: Time will take care of everything. You'll see.

YOUNG MAN: You're talking in circles.

OLD MAN: Wisdom comes in circles. Time comes in circles. I talk to bring you around.

YOUNG MAN: I think I shall die. Your words mean nothing to me. My heart aches and time is cruel for it has stopped. I want to die.

OLD MAN: Then DIE, GODDAMMIT!!! And then time will have taken care of everything.

POLITICIAN

Rigger raff, mish mash
Acrobatic lip lash
Rumba tumba mumba jumba
Twiddle dee dee bo bash

Bicker bucker, hand shucker
Smiley whiley bite
Promise ooh, promise aah
Wriggly miggly mite

He magician, funny fiction
Tickadee tackadee tongue
Frumble clapper, flipper flapper
Doubledee dealin' in dung

Juggledeedoo, plug leakadeeho
Cover up lover up pay
Tippadee toein', snow jobadee blowin'
Tomorrow can pay for today

Bickerdee bucker, he eagle plucker
Sell store before he'd agree
Egoplastic, split tongue and elastic
Pour honey to what crowd he see

Politician, steal technician
Circledee talkadee jerky
Overhaul law to fit in his craw
A genuine national turkey

Can't agreebadeedoo, can't agreebadeedo
Dividing the house against self
Rather sell out the race than agree and lose face
Rather freedom be put on a shelf

But harkadeedoo, harkadeeho
Send out the word by land and by sea

continued . . .

In spite of confusion and justice occlusion
There's something on which they agree!

(What be this strange dance?
Why now their embrace?
Bedfellows smiling,
They gladly give face,
No confusion, no confusion,
When they're hooking up for a money transfusion!

What stilled stormy waters?
What smoothed out their sail?
They're hugging, high fiving
And lifting their ale:
No confusion, just collusion—to buy a double
Shot of votes and get a money transfusion!)

Yes, send out the word by land and by sea
There's something on which they all agree:
No confusion, no confusion,
Let's see how they get their money transfusion:

See the Doctors of Law
Fix it up right?
See the Surgeons of Justice
Work through the night?

(I can't believe what I do see!
They're moving in perfect harmony!)

So the call goes out to get a raise
And to be exempt from the tax
And the voices ring out, "Aye! Aye! Aye! Aye!"
Their purpose is right on track.

• • • • • • • • • •

The Doctor of Law is tax exempt
EE I EE I O

continued . . .

With a quack quack here and a quack quack there
The Doctor of Law is tax exempt
EE I EE LOOPHOLE

Ol' McCongressman got a raise
EE I EE I O
With an oink oink here and an oink oink there
Ol' McCongressman got a raise
AYE! QUACK! OINK! I OWE!

AND THE BEAT GOES ON: JULY 20, 1969

The Eagle descends.
A shivering baby cries from hunger in Bigtown, USA
    and a man lies drunk in the street.

A man fishing looks at the rising moon
    and wonders if they're there yet.
The river flows and the moon shines
And the Eagle still descends.

(Some people are saying the end will come now
    because man will step foot on the moon.
What's the relationship?
A little boy crosses the street for the first time.
In 1492, Columbus sailed . . .)

A boy and a girl in a parked car are breathing heavily.
The wind blows a branch against the window.
The boy looks up and notices the moon.
He says: "Wonder if they're there yet?"
She says: "If you'd get a radio for this stupid car,
        you'd know. Anyway, who cares?"
The boy wraps back around her smiling.
Heavy breathing again.
The Eagle descends.
She says: "You're all hands and tongue tonight!"
He says: "That's what separates man from the beasts!"
She says: "You are a beast."
He says: "And you tempt the beast."
The moon is sure bright tonight.
A coyote howls.
Heavy breathing.
The Eagle descends.

• • • • • • • • • •

A car hits a car and a life fades to nothing.
Someone's world ends.

continued . . .

A woman cries in numbness and a doctor
    pumps her full of numbing drugs.

She can't live without her husband.
She tells herself this over and over.
Why isn't once enough?
The human mind is stubborn.
The human mind is plastic.
The human mind evolves and flows
    on and on
        and a man eats a man
            along the Amazon
                and the Eagle touches down.
The moon didn't turn red.

A mosquito bites the man fishing
    and he raises his hand to slap
    but a fish strikes and he forgets the mosquito
        and he forgets the moon.

My God! A human being is walking on the moon!
My God! A human being used to be some sort of fish!
It was a long journey to the moon.

• • • • • • • • • •

The baby's crying, Fred!
What's for supper tonight?
Hey! Can I borrow some Scotch tape?
And the Lord said: "A new and greater commandment
        I give unto you . . ."
We're in Vietnam to . . .
I'm getting a new Corvette tomorrow!
I want to go to heaven, but I don't want to die . . .
Some of my best friends are . . .
The Kingdom of Heaven is within you . . .
Burn her! She's a witch!
For God and Country.
God is an American, said the American.

continued . . .

God is a Turk, said the Turk.
God is a German, said the German.
God is Chinese, said the Chinaman.
God is a sea gull, said Johnathan Livingston.
God is fed up, said the man in the moon.

The boy in the parked car looks back at the moon.
Neil Armstrong's feet are moving on the surface.
She says: "Let's head back now. We went far enough . . .
    it scared me."

Hickory dickory dock,
The mouse couldn't turn back the clock.
Now the mouse is gone and time moves on
Calling shots from the auction block.

A baby shivers and cries from hunger in Smalltown, USA
    and a man lies drunk in the street.
Someone is blaming Neil Armstrong for that.
It's a sin to be curious, some say.
Science is God's foe,
Even though the old lady put down her Bible
    to watch the news of the Ted Kennedy scandal
        glow from the fluorescent screen before
            going to the cupboard for her medicine.

• • • • • • • • • •

And the prophet said:
    "Feed them and care for them until
    they are liken to the fat cattle of the field,
    And the cow will never jump over the moon."

CAGES

On a Florida swamp tour
On a boat called Jungle Queen
Many people went with cameras
So they could impress friends
With where they had been
        and what they had seen.

The boat stopped at a rest station
Where black squirrels, parrots, gators,
And a variety of jungle animals
Were unconsciously entertaining
        from within their cages.

A Seminole man wrestled
A doped-up gator and
Held him in position
    for the cameras: CLICK! CLICK! CLICK!

When time was running short
Some very young Seminole children
Sang Jesus Loves Me and
Said the I Pledge Allegiance.
All this was to the delight of
Old rich women
        with blue hair and pink faces
Who chuckled and went on about
        how cute it all was.

Then the tin cups sitting in front of the children
Gave out an occasional CLANK! CLANK! CLANK!
As the coins dropped in—
Falling hard and evident
    like a burden falling from a bothered conscious.
The coins once given
    rewrapped pink cotton around
        the givers' minds.

continued . . .

When the boat pulled away
All the passengers looked at the Indians
        waving a well rehearsed goodbye,

And they waved back smiling
        for they had been pleased.

And as the boat pulled further away,
One could look back and see
The animals—
In their cages
And the Indians—

A QUEEN'S THRONE ON A BROKEN BUS

All she wanted was a seat.
All she wanted, to rest her feet.
All she wanted—what we all want:
A gentle stroke to the soul from the immediate world around.

But the whole weight of Ownership and Control
Was laying on her pretty hatted head,
Saying, "KNOW YOUR PLACE!"

Truth was, she did know.
Like a flower opening up to the light
Of the big grand sky knows its place,
She knew hers.

Told to give up her seat,
She remained seated.
Told, "Well, I'm going to have you arrested."
She, with a gentle voice absent of rage or malice,
Spoke like a sweet holy distant thunder
Rolling down through the ages
                    cleansing, softly cleansing,
Saying: "You may go on and do so."

And with those words, resigned to whatever
                    may come of it,
She leaned gently against a South wind
That still stank of antebellum stagnation,
Still stank with the faint scent of whips
And ropes and chains.

Gently speaking, gently leaning,
Dignity and Grace crowned a Queen that day,
As her courage lifted the night.
This is a praise I sing to thee—Dear
Sweet Rosa.

THE MAY 4TH MASSACRE
Kent State University

Peace was failing
Souls were wailing
Over new war action
A new unveiling
Of a new reaction.

Bad winds blown
Stones were thrown
Both sides were right
So bravery had grown
And they made their fight.

Some rounds were fired
Some souls retired
They lay like stones
In the street and yard
Something's wrong.

• • • • • • • • • •

"The strength of our country lies
in our educational institutions . . . and on and on . . .
The fighting men and women who serve our country at
home and abroad to keep us free, carry with them the
hearts of all Americans and our deepest appreciation for
their noble job . . . and on and on . . ."

The man in the suit on the TV screen sitting between two American flags has a good writer as thinking people sit and listen numbly as he goes on and on and on.

• • • • • • • • • •

KNOCK ON THE DOOR—STATE POLICE:

"Are you Mr. and Mrs. So and So?
We regret to inform you that your daughter was shot

continued . . .

to death while demonstrating on campus against the U.S.'s recent action in Cambodia. . . ."

The slow, Tic Toc, growing, eating pain song
                    starts in the parents' brains.
They stare with stone eyes
                    into their brains
At the big, stone hard, jagged WHY? that will
Never be answered.
Tic, Toc, Tic. . . .
And the song goes on.

• • • • • • • • • •

"Hey Joe! Read that new book?"
"Which one?"
"The Rise And Fall Of The American Empire."
"No, I think it would bore me."
"Maybe, but it's pretty interesting . . . it's got a lot
of gory stuff in it."

• • • • • • • • • •

Why? Why?—Whatever happened—?
Where was the tear gas?
The mace, the fire hose?
Who called the shots?
Nobody knows. And
Whatever happened to America is
        a question reflected from glazed eyes
As they lay like stones
                    in the street and yard—
Tic, Toc, Tic

TO RUSSIA WITH LOVE: A COLD WAR TIMEPIECE JUNE 1982

Dear Russia
Please open up your ears
It's way beyond who's right or wrong
Or any childhood fears

I ain't criticizin' Karl Marx
Or the brand of chains you wear
I ain't trying to sell you God
Amway or Tupperware

Dear Russia
Please open up your eyes
We surely have a higher purpose
Than poisoning the skies

Listen Yuri, listen Laura
Our babes will cry out loud
When all we have to offer them
Is the crop from a mushroom cloud

It's too late in the day for bombs away
For Hitler or John Wayne
It's not enough just to be tough
We also must be sane

You think your wheat crop looks bad now?
And the economy is lame?
You won't know hell 'til you try to eat
After radioactive rain

CHORUS:

> Dear Russia
> Let's not let our children die
> Let's let 'em grow and let 'em know
> That blue's still the color of the sky
>
> Let's let 'em be and let 'em see
> That green's still the color of the grass

continued . . .

Let's gather up all the poison bombs
And shove 'em up the devil's ass

What I'm sayin' concerns us all
We're livin' off the same sweet tit
As long as Earth is still our home
We'd better take care of it

We can squabble and squander and bitch and rave
And cuss 'til we're blue in the face
But if we fight on a cliff and both of us slip
It's curtains for the human race

REPEAT CHORUS

SONGBOOK

THE CLOCK

That clock on the wall
I don't understand at all
I sit and watch the movement of the hands
As they climb and fall

It reminds me of the past and tomorrow
But the face is still the same
Is it my face I see and the face I see
Never seems to change

CHORUS:

It seems that it means nothing
To watch my life go passing
To the beat of the ticking of the clock
How can my life change
When the numbers are arranged
In a circle, you end up where you start

I think about a girl
Who now belongs to yesterday
And the hands on the clock keep pushing
Her further away

With my mind my hopes keep flirtin'
But I'm tired of this run around game
And if time keeps bringin' nothin'
I know I'm gonna go insane

CHORUS:

And as the clock turns around
And the leaves turn to brown
I'm sittin' here wondering in the night
Will the clock on the wall
Stop me from my fall
And let me see the mornin' light?
And let me see the mornin' light?
Please let me see the mornin' light

TRIP TO FLORIDA SONG

Bonita, where did you go?
I miss receiving that smile that I know.
Bonita, where are you now?
I heard you moved where the hurricanes howl.

Bonita, what do you do?
Are your days comin' easy,
Are you gonna make it through?
Bonita, so full of life,
I can't help but hopin'
No man's took you for his wife.

CHORUS:

I think I'll take a hitchhike
I've nothing else at hand,
And comb the warm white beaches
Barefooted in the sand.

I'll lay away a day or two
With a bottle and a song,
I'll try to sing away the blue
And the hurt of what went wrong.

And if by chance I come across
An old friend that I knew,
I've got to say Bonita,
I'm hopin' that it's you.

If we meet again
I hope I don't scare you away.
I'm not on my knees to beg
And take you away.

Bonita, I've not much on my mind,
I'd like to spend a day
And see your smile one more time.

REPEAT CHORUS

SAIL ON, SAIL ON

Something from a way way long time ago
Something deep down in your bones
Something going on when people speak tongues
And let spirit set fire to their songs

It's something clear from the dark side of time
And so near you don't even know it
It's something will take your heart for a ride
You reap it without having sown it

It's something from a way way long time ago
That nursed the birth of mankind
From the time spirit moved through water and clay
And blew us right into our mind

Something that turns the seasons around
Chips crystals of snow from the air
Fruit, color, creation—tomorrow's vibration
Locked safely within the seed's care

Something from a way long long time ago
That's pushin' the blood through your veins
Why eyes can read the structure of light
Why skies can send down the rain

Something from a long long long time ago
Nourishes you while you sleep
A light bursting through the top of your head
Coming from down in the deep

A crystal clear reason spoke purpose to soul
And set fire in Michelangelo's hand
Mozart played keys that could break hearts of stone
The sea sings boulders to sand

Something from a way way long time ago
Something deep down in your bones

continued . . .

Something from a way way long time ago
Sail on   sail on

Something from a way way long time ago
Sail on   sail on
Something from a way way long time ago
Sail on   sail on

ODE TO PEOPLE WHO DON'T LIKE THEIR PARENTS

You can blame 'em, insane 'em,
You can slander and de-fame 'em
Kill 'em or sue 'em,
Or maybe even want to screw 'em.

You can ignore 'em, deplore 'em,
Go find a home in which to store 'em
Or you can strip 'em, you can whip 'em,
You can drive 'em nuts and then commit 'em.

CHORUS:

I don't care what you do
There's a little bit of Ma and Pa
in me and you.
You can't escape, it's part of your fate
You're busy laughin' at them
they're busy bein' you.

You gotta face it, you can't escape it
A change of name just won't erase it
You're daddy's temper, your mama's fat,
Go look in the mirror that's exactly where you're at.

You can expose 'em or decompose 'em,
Keep your friends away so noone knows 'em
Then fake a cry at their death bed
Hopin' they'll forgive and leave you all their bread.

REPEAT CHORUS

BLACK BOTTOM BABY

Black bottom baby
I love your African ass
Black bottom baby
I love your African ass
Dark flame dancin' in the moonlight
Come lay it down in the grass

Sweet jungle Angel
Your lips the texture of love
Sweet jungle Angel
Your lips the texture of love
They must've blown down from Heaven
They fit like a glove

Black diamond eyes
Look straight to my soul
Black diamond eyes
Look straight into my soul
I want to be your midnight slave
Come make me rock and roll

Sweet rhythmic heat
Wrap your wings around me
Sweet rhythmic heat
Wrap your wings around me
I want to be your work of art
Black velvet and free

REPEAT FIRST VERSE

IT WAS YOU, AFTER ALL

Your Daddy was a Kodiak fisherman
With blue runnin' through his veins
His voice was weak but his thoughts held you
Pulling gently like his seines

Your momma drank a little too much
Workin' on disrepair
Temper and fire kept the boys away
They called her the Russian Bear

Your Daddy was a Kodiak fisherman
With salt runnin' through his veins
Livin' and workin' up and down the swells
I don't even think he knew my name

One day I braved to knock your door
Your Momma met me right there
Whatever I said must've been right
She opened up her lair

CHORUS:

How I love to think of those days
When the island sparkled in sunlight
Or wore a shroud of a misty haze

1. Feelin' free and crazy to run
   Down the shore to that little white house
   To feel the warmth of the sun

2. Feelin' free and feelin' so glad
   Runnin' down the shore to that little white house
   To feel the warmth of everything you had
   It was you, after all, it was you

You were the daughter of a fisherman
With love runnin' through your veins

continued . . .

Life was the sea you sailed upon
Joy was your bounty main

You had a little of your Momma's fire
A little of her temper too
Though your eyes were brown they revealed a hint
Of a wild and windy blue

I knew at the time my heart was fire
Lovin' life inside and out
But I didn't know how, I didn't know why
Or what it was all about

Why do I love the mountains
And the deep dark stormy blue?
Now I see it all 'cause after all
I see it all through you

REPEAT CHORUS

MIDDLE AGE CRAZIES

I got the middle age crazies
And I wonder if I'm gonna make it through
I thought by now I'd have some answers
To at least a heavy question or two
But I swear by the air that I'm breathin'
I don't know if I'm arrivin' or leavin'
But these middle age crazies
Keep me rockin' and rollin' with you

Still like to catch a buzz
Still like to shake the bedroom walls
Still like playin' my guitar
Still like playin' basketball
But nothin' looks quite the same
When you're halfway through the game
Runnin' crazy like it's Spring
When you know that it's damn near Fall

CHORUS

Got the middle age crazies
Got those halfway blues
Everybody's wearin' cowboy boots
And steppin' on my blue suede shoes
Everything keeps changin' so fast
I just don't know how much longer I'll last
But these middle age crazies
Keep me rockin' and rollin' with you

I still look at all the women
They could lock me up for what's in my head,
But I'm thinkin' that the day I stop lookin'
Is the day that I'm dead
I'm appreciatin' everything more
But I'm takin' it a little bit slower
Cause my mind is full of ideas
But my ass is full of lead

REPEAT CHORUS

BEWARE THE COMFORT OF SELF-DESTRUCTION

You just wanna go to sleep
With music playin' in your ears
It feels so good just to let it all go
And not face up to what you're here for

CHORUS:

So easy, so easy
It feels so good and so easy
But you might as well sit around and hit yourself
Right in the head with a hammer
Then grin at each other while you pay the price
Of the comfort of self-destruction

It's easy puttin' off to death
What you can do to life
Let 'em take the cold shower away
Come back and wake you another day

CHORUS:

It's easy, so easy
Ridin' the ship Anesthesia
But you might as well drill through the top of your head
And pour hot tar in your brain
Then grin and pass it while you fall in love
With the comfort of self-destruction

Television's all you need
You hope the telephone won't ring
It's kinda rough talkin' when you barely are thinkin'
It feels like floatin' but you know you're sinkin'

CHORUS:

It's easy, so easy
Givin' up is so easy
But you might as well wave a little white flag
And tie sand bags to your heart

continued . . .

Then lie there and hide there and curl up like a fetus
In the comfort of self-destruction

You wanna play away the day
Thinkin' time will never end
Ignorin' the direction that you are goin'
Never payin' mind to what you're reapin' or you're sowin'

CHORUS:

It's easy, so easy
Self inflicted amnesia
But you might as well shoot broken glass in your veins
And go to bed without a reason to rise
Listen to me children, it ain't no good
The comfort of self-destruction

Had to try my hand at a country song at least once, so here it is. . . .

WHEN YOU'RE FEELIN' NO PAIN

I woke up and hurt
'cause the woman I love
Is gone
And I cannot forget her

Had breakfast with hurt
Tried to read the sports
But she's gone
And I cannot forget her

Went to work and hurt
Tried to concentrate
But it's hard
When I'm thinking about her

After work, still hurt
So I seek relief
Goin' fast
And double on whiskey

CHORUS:

It's easy to forget the blue
So easy when you're feelin' no pain
Forgettin' about the hurt that you feel
Is so easy when you're feelin' no pain

Woke up and hurt
'cause the woman I love
Is gone
And I cannot forget her

REPEAT CHORUS TWICE

LEAVES TURN BROWN

Time, stay a little longer
Wind, blow fresh air my way
Girl, give me all your lovin'
And all my friends come visit me today

Time, give to me some answers
Wind, don't let my world grow stale
Girl, will you be there tomorrow?
And will my friends be friends if I should fail?

CHORUS:

I really want to live with all my might
There's nothing I want to miss
(I can't sleep at night)

What life is all about I'll never know
But I know I want to stay
(Don't want to go
Don't want to go
Don't want to go)

Time, I know you have restrictions
Wind, I know sometimes you wail
Girl, I know you need your own time
And friends may catch a different wind to sail

REPEAT CHORUS

Time, don't be so apathetic
Wind, you're loafin' on the way
Girl, you seem to be so moody
And no friends came to visit me today

LAY DOWN BESIDE ME

I can see
A load of worry in your eyes
And a load of sorrow weighin' on your head
I can see
You're carryin' the whole day long
On your shoulders

Take it off
Take it all off
And lay down beside me

Take it off
Take it all off
And lay down beside me

CHORUS:

You're wearin'
A sad time on your head
You're carryin'
A bad day on your shoulders
You're bearin' a load
That you can unload on me
Take it off
Take it all off
And lay down beside me
Take it off
Take it all off
And lay down beside me

The road you've walked
Is a rocky one I know
You're heart is tired, in need of rest
Feel free,
To take cool drink from my well
And unload all your cares

continued . . .

Take it off
Take it all off
And lay down beside me

Take it off
Take it all off
And lay down beside me